AF596172

IN BLOOD I WROTE

SYLVESTER STEVEN WRIGHT "WRITTEN LUV"

EYE OF THE BEHOLDER VISUAL ARTS PUBLISHING

IN BLOOD I WROTE

 Printed in the United States of America.
For information PLEASE EMAIL eyeofthebeholdervisualarts@gmail.com or sylvesterstevenwrightauthor@gmail.com.

ISBN

DEDICATION

Oki,

I dedicate this book to my grandfather Lester Wright, father and business owner. I also dedicate this book to my mother Christine Wright and my sister Trenise Shanoil Anderson. We haven't spoken in years but you are where I learned to love black women and where I learned to let them go. My first loves.

To my ex wife Katrina and mother to my beautiful son, I thank you for everything good and bad. We are always family.

To my heart, my soul and the love of my life Robin Michelle Gannaway, who through this poetry of prayers is the answer to my dreams.

To my best friend so close we called each other cousins. We fought, each other and anyone who tried us we were vicious. You passed and I miss you but thank you for making me a better man you and your brother Patrick, Danica and Carletha. I love you Kumar you are music see you in eternity.

Purposely last and in no way least, Lisa M. Forbes aka Concise, the main and only reason the book was done. We had a lot of bitter fights but in the end I have learned and I am still learning so much from you. Thank you for all that you have done.

To all here I love you always and thank you for your addition to my heart on paper. I dedicate this to all black women and men, to all people and all ethnicities.

To life, love, lust and the courage to write your heart out so the world can see for eternity.

Fah Pahnomcinfu Terinometa,

Sylvester

PREFACE

"In Blood I Wrote" formerly called "Less Traveled the Road" and publish in 2009, to put into words what this book is about is not hard at all. These words represent my desire, my wish to be loved and adored by black women. My wish to be listened to and admired by black men as a model, "Yes, I am vain." These words are my prayer for bitter love that has never been seen, "love unconditional." In Blood I Wrote, is my cry to be better and love me better. These are my words to the courageous women who are beautiful in all ways. This is my plea to all the Gwendolyn Brooks' of the world to be a shining light once again, Afros, Dreads, Nappy, Bald Heads, to be the norm not permed knots and so forth. This is my way of asking to be a better person, to make this a better world—a trutopia. I love language, the ability to take that which has no life and make it Dance. This book in a nutshell is my heart and desire, this is personal. Every poem has a story—love, lust and knowledge. I only hope you enjoy it as much as I have and still do. Thank You

Written Love

The messages are so untouched, unrehearsed and profound.
You know the way the pen, the pencil, the pad compound?
Their one word is a sentence, describing nouns.
How do they get so deep down in the crevice of written love?

I am lost in the use of words with deferred meanings.
These actions, pictures in letters that should mean nothing,
yet given life by sweet rainbow lips.
Written love from enlightened fingertips.

I am the luckiest to see the ability of their written love, when it is not solely confined within me, but shared freely with my community.
Yet within the radius of love written so deep for life even in the hurt and pain felt, we share these words true as the blood of ourselves.
Written love.

It takes honesty to share one's heart, guts, veins, brain and soul.
Sharing sicknesses, hatreds and oppressions,
learned life lessons, stupidities and ideologies.
Putting it all on a plate for the world to judge, digest and possibly regurgitate.
Written love.

I am lost in the words of love, the words of hate, and the words of knowledge.
I am lost in the words of humanity, philosophy, and insanity,
the vanity of the vain to write the truth and bear the pain and scrutiny of society.
To say "fuck them all," I am refusing to be anything less than me.
This is the power of,
Written love.

Word Play

She came to me when I was about 2 or 3

saying, “Be my pimp use my letters to set minds free,

but be loyal to me and I will always be in you.”

So I thought about her offer until the dawn.

But why do I need her when in truth with these words I am Bishop Don Juan?

And so of course I cheated and I mixed, tricked these letters out and shit.

Life is a bitch, and these letters help my soul deal with it.

So I asked, “How with all these possibilities am I supposed

to wed my temporal lobes, to only you, your words and your fold?

I’d be a fool a pimp with no...Well damn you know!”

She smiled and she laughed in many different sounds cast

from her lips that could stop sound in mid sentence.

Well you know I had to be me pimped out with these words,

mastering these nouns and verbs. She was still laughing she had not heard.

But before I could speak this... well you know.

She spoke softness from head to toe. I’m talking pimp game so solid it would

Word Play

Sink,

not float, full proof pimp, she had a swagger with a slight limp.

She explained, "In the midst of hordes of pain,

I am not words, they are a piece of my herd."

"What are you then and why should you be my only friend?"

"I am more than mere sound, more than how your words get down."

"What are you then and why should you be all that I live in?"

She smiled and said, "Baby listen I am not words but language. I am not language but culture. I am not culture but humanity. I am not humanity but humanity's creativity. You can never cheat on me you can never forsake me. I am the expression of words and the writing of words. You are a mere sheep in the flock I am the entire herd, word!" "Word?" She spoke to me of the Poetry of Life and she made me understand, I never pimped these words I

MADE THEM MY WIFE!

Tall Talk

"Brotha you got a long, fat, chocolate sleek sweet tasting treat, my ear drums slurp down your release," she said.

"What?"

"I mean it goes so deep it stretches my intellect to its maximum!" She said.

"HUH?"

"Listen! It touches me immensely!" She said.

"What?"

"Listen! It's that African drum deepness shaking my cervix its width and length are infinite. My eyes lose focus, my throat loses air, that's why only screams are there!" she said.

"What?"

"Listen! You move me and my insides deeply my ear drums cum knowledge."

"Listen!"

Finally I heard she wasn't talking 'bout my dick she was talking 'bout my words.

Hear Me Roar

Listen, you can say what you want about me just as long as you don't get on this here poetry. Can you feel these words addictive like crack? Heroine to your veins, actually heroine to your brains? These words that fill my soul when all else fails, that move my blindness from Braille. I wield the mightiest sword known to man...the steel? No the pen or the pencil, like the edge of shut doors and window sills, like picture stills. Baby for real, I am the real deal. After me there is none who can fill these size twelve and a half's. My words have swollen until my pen has lost control and has burst like lungs with too much air. Like a skunk sprays its funk I fill the air. Can you feel me there? Can you hear me dear? Let me slide something nice and hard yet soft and wet in your ear. Let me make your mind cum, fuck the body. Let me make your soul explode in multitudes of joy. Oh boy! Where my body may fail you, where my tricks may not overwhelm you, allow my mind to astound you, and all else will be but a distant memory as if from a past love. Let me be the last thing you think of when you sleep, breathe me in deep. Allow my mental endowment between the lips on your chin. Let me have mental intercourse beyond all you can comprehend.

Hear Me Roar

My only mission? To take you higher, no to take you beyond that where there is no existence, and yes I will be persistent. Offer me all your resistance. Let me break your walls. Let me show you love in a different, uncorrupted way. Fuck my size and how I can be divine between your thighs. Let me touch your mind leaving our bodies so far behind that we exist outside of time. I promise never to fail you, my words will never derail you, they will always be true, and do the things they say they will do. Oh, you want to kiss my lips? No let me kiss your mind and watch how much deeper, how much sweeter it can be bringing tears of joy you deserve. Let my mental tongue elevate your soul high, so high that heaven is beneath you. These words I speak true. Listen beautiful, to hell with the body let's see what our minds can do. Let my eternal journey be your explosion. Your essence losing composition, listen allow me access to the depth of your stress beyond and past your cervix. Now that we're done was it worth it?

Hear me roar.

Warning! If you are close to the one you love this poem may excite you to nymphomania. If you are taking any drugs that alter the senses, it is advised to wait three days as this poem is so hot it may cause severe hallucinations. And if you have a heart condition well you gone die anyway so look at this as dying on top of your fine ass woman during…well you figure it out!

Lost In Vocalization

Baby listen…whatever your name is, I am sweet like center stage and showbiz. Word genius, rhythm wiz, they like is that slang his? Hey! Is that the kid who wrote those words so big? Or is he just another clone? Listen Miss I can make panties so wet they no longer absorb cum. I can make women smile so much their cheeks tighten from too much fun. I can turn that weak ass, always last, ignored by the masses, into your prince charming. I am king rhythm lost in rhyming but caught in timing. I am truth. I am the doctor of sex something to make her tight legs loose. I am however not the so-called doctor Seuss. My long term goal? To study breaking the mold. I am forever telling them to grab a hold and don't let go. This is for all people, my nation.

Don't get lost in the vocalization!

Dude listen to me bring your pimpology, I am the student and master of wordology. I am the perfection of noun, verb and sentence chemistry. My words are the mystery still unsolved, not because they choose to be, but because you lack true individuality to see past the box. Confined and doomed I will free you like perming dreaded locks. Like smelly feet freed from sweating socks. Like time released from a stagnant clock. I am the word. Do not confuse that with the religious absurd. I am the sentence…perfect. I am the drop in a base line with beats that are so worth it. For you to dance to I am the perfect rhythm, sound. This is how I get down. Hold on for a ride out of your localization, but if you fall you are forever lost in vocalization!

Lost In Vocalization

Listen princess you have never truly cum, but if you follow these words I can make you fall like flood watch rain. I can make all your mounds of pain release and with this power all I ask is for peace. All I ask is for release. Woman listen, I am beauty, that perfect booty, the perfect butterfly. I am not talking about the bug but how she winds her hips in that dance of love. I am those curves that make her shape hour glass. I am the future, the present and the good and bad of the past. I am that thing in your talk that makes her look at you, that shake in your walk that makes him want you, that is what I am. You need a reason to smile? Sniff these words and lick these chocolate lips. I submit just this here guarantee, there will never be words written or combined like me.

Lost in vocalization!

Calling Me

I hear you calling me mother Africa not the land…the culture

I hear you calling me back to the spear

Back to the chase of the gazelle like deer

I hear Africa call me not the tribe not the king

The poor war torn ones that sing

I hear you calling me back to the shield

Back to the field

Where sticks we wield

To fight off lions from the skins of our young

I hear the sound of drums not of the warrior

We are so much more

The riddle cry of the witch doctor

Belly dancers, all dancers throwing their feet to the blue white skies

Calling the dead and me

Calling Me

I hear the sweet soft voice with the strength of the word

Before religion made us one of the herd

I hear you calling me from the bush not the African one

The ones on Crenshaw and Stocker

I hear you scream at the top of your lungs

Freedom

You call me to conform as a slave

I hear you calling me screaming the names the slave owner gave me

Who penetrated not just your vaginas but pushed deep into your culture

Your idea of me, you, us, we

I hear you calling me to join you

Shun me with no love when and if I refuse to do what you want me to

I still love you

I hear you calling me whispering…sweet stares my way

I hear you calling me

However my name is not n@#$* and I am no kin to conformity

Home Bound

I was on my way home, bound to the red, black and green. Got sidetracked on my way back now as an American my soul dreams. My bus was hijacked around Western and Florence by European ignorance. Laid like laws in accordance to this idea of being better than you, ¾ of a man we are considered bipedal chimpanzees in tuxedos. Entertaining this world with animal deeds, can I sing to you? Or maybe do a tap dance or two? Don't need to paint my face just draw the lips white. We give you constant ethnic slurs and imitations for your delight. I was trying to advance my experience, but when they shot Martin that day they took away not only my innocence but my common sense.

Now each day I wake is classically spent trying to free myself from poverty. I spend all my money trying to prove to bumblebees I have honey. It makes no sense that I can afford hairdos and rims but daddy can't make the rent. I am the bastard great grand child of slaves. My ignorance is to the 10th power. I have laid my seed with booze and weed. I acquired that over bearing need to be told how to proceed. My life is lived like a parasite being eaten on by parasites living as a stereotype. This was once a lie now a truth, I am home bound but I will never get through.

The Dream

I dreamed of uniting Africa. Back to when being African was all that mattered and tribalism was the idea of the stupid and hateful, but it was just an idea. I dreamed of uniting each tribe into a nation, under one idea, that being the love of life above all other ideas. I dreamed of African kings throwing their crowns to the people in a gesture that would wipe out class-ism. I dreamed of Africa united under one government, where every citizen's voice was heard, where the majority and the minority did not exist. I dreamed of the bloodshed in the uniting of Africa, because some would rather use their power to build and some would listen to no reason and destroy all will. I have seen the death of leaders who valued position over life, soldiers who were loyal to kings not to the idea of humanity and a life of fighting for peace. I dreamed of children dying, mothers crying because men refused to acknowledge defeat at the hands of life's truths. I dreamed of mighty nations drawing arms for fear of a black super power because all they would see was another threat. But in the end it was not because I dreamed of smiling eyes that cried joyous tears that Africa was united. It was because men valued something bigger than themselves, something bigger than philosophy. I dreamed for the advancement of my people mentally, spiritually and physically. I dedicate this wholeheartedly to my people, the human race!

Message in a Body

I send this to you my love, you may not know but there was a time when men of all colors, ethnicities and ideologies roamed free. It was before the continental drift, before the unnamed god separated Babylon, before even monotheism. I write this to you my love from the *Mayflower* on the loin cloth of my deceased brother with his blood. I will place it in his abdomen next to his heart so that you will know your story. I hope the body will preserve long enough to reach land without decay, so that way, the dry coagulated words written won't wash away. I love you. When men speak of Africa they will try to make it black, they will try to say that time away is why you have these different skin colors today. It is a lie. When they talk about Africa they will try to make it savage, ignorant it is a lie. When they talk about Africa they will try to say we are the closest descendents to apes and that their ancestors traveled to the North, and that is where they became light, it is a lie. They will call themselves civilized, learned or educated. It is a lie do not be a victim of it. When they talk about humanity they will say things like the white race or black race these are lies used to hurt and separate. The truth is when they came back to Africa they saw men as light as them. They killed them all so no one would know the truth. Africa is not a color, it is a community of humanity. I know they will throw his body overboard soon. My color, my love, is black as night. My dead brother he was white. Remember love, it may be a little hard but if you find him look in his ribcage the message is hidden in place of his heart.

Yours truly,

Brother

Rusting Chains

They picked me up on the western shore, right before the open door to Africa. I was somewhere around Kenya with my Mama and my Baba sitting, eating a dish from the Zulu. I ask of you, "Who knew they took me?" I was smuggled along the trails of the slave trade where white men learned Swazi to help with the selling. They would thoroughly check my teeth as if I were a horse, "buck" they would call me. My mother and father jumped overboard but the thief kept me. I was not allowed the choice of death over slavery. I was shackled and chained, whipped 'til I bled from my brain. I was then taught a systems philosophy and now some lost soul tells me to let it be. They say that the past was slavery. Then I ask cordially, "If so why is it they still have crackers on horse back? Why do they still crack backs with night sticks, instead of whips, chewing tobacco with ethnic slurs they spit? Why am I still living in poverty?" It is the same as when they had slaves in slavery. Why is my color still an issue? If I am a man why do you continue to refer to me as buck, or animalistic terms that suck? Why does your law not apply to me, if I am a human and that is what you see?

Somewhere along the outhouse of the Virginia slave master's mansion as I picked cotton from cotton fields, I chanced to meet an old man from the old country. He was not conditioned though living in submission. His words swift and clear, his hollow eyes spoke of no fear. I asked him, "Why are you here?" He said, "Yes it is true, I am here just as the others too, but sit down young crown I endured this waiting for you." His words were like hot pokes to my head.

Rusting Chains

"It is a system of control. It confines the mind, the heart and chains the soul. Soon it will be all you know. I am here to give you so much more so that you grow." The rusty chain still hung around his neck, but his head was held proud with self respect. He said, "I am freedom. My name came before the mass enslavement, it is not a product of hatred. It is the will and the natural desire to achieve higher. I am the African spear, the shield, the garment. I am history still in the making. I am freedom. Read between the lines of heretics before they forget their lies. I am the music of African drums. I stand not side by side with the lion, I am the lion. I am freedom. Remember me and remember being free!"

I ran that day from the man on the horse swinging his whip at me. I ran as fast as my legs could take me but I was alone. Freedom was not at my side he chose to remain behind. I was just a child lucky to be alive. Sticking to the back roads and the woods, meeting runners like me who told me of a promised land where slaves could be free. I followed underground railroads and months of conspiracy. Yet I wondered why when I ran did freedom not follow me? I could still see his hollow eyes smiling as I ran. However no one else seemed to bother this seemingly defiant man. He smiled as I out paced the horses chase. I could even hear him scream, "Even when you are bound down keep a smile on your face!" But I have wondered even to this day why he never came with his young pupil to flee, and only now do I realize he was not at my side because freedom was within me.

That day I broke those rusty chains, but the loss and the pain still remain.

Fear Dom

Damn it's scary to see their brains at work for fear they may try walking and thinking at the same time, trip and get hurt, there's that silence again, the blinking eyes of the intellectually thin, and how smart are we, to let them control everything, blink turn left, drink turn right, fall because their feet aren't right, or too much light, and not enough sense to avert their eyes, no they stare right into the light, and wonder why they can't steer their cars right, and which way is left?

Change for a Dollar Please

It is so sadly stated that money is the root of all evil.
Many will tell you that its roots are so deep in the soul the two can't be separated.
I ask, "What about that cash makes women shake their asses?"
I ask, "What about that dough made her change the locks in her fro?"
It is put so eloquently for the world to hear not see,
make the cash, don't make the cash your last.

So I stand next to the music with diamonds that glitter,
with my pants sagging down looking at girls like come hither.
While the block I grew up on dies eternally and withers,
while men destroy lives like snakes that slither.

I ask, "Can I have change for a dollar?"
Some may not understand the metaphor and if I give the answer,
they'd understand it less not more.
Oh yes, by the way, the answer is no.
I ask, "Do you understand the words I've spoken?"
You live like a king yet you are forever broke and broken.

Change for a Dollar Please

I ask, "Can I have change for a dollar?"
Your eyes glaze as they focus in on what your ears are hearing.
Hell no! You can't get change for a dollar.
In fact you can't get change for a million dollars,
since it is a fact that money does not change you.

Money can't make you better wiser or smarter.
Money can't help you grow, not in the ways that count.
Money can't buy you anything to free your mind.
Money can't help your smoked out brain see that your ass is blind.

So what would you do for a little change?
Shake your ass on a stage or blow out a man's brains?
Would you sell your family to slave owners for gain?
Would you even straighten your hair and lose your ethnic mane?

Listen to me, "Change for a dollar please?"
Can't get change for a dollar because money don't change you.

Clarity

I am literally beside myself, standing in amazement at your wealth.
Lost in the strength of your health, captivated by the bounty of beauty
that is sent like shock waves to all paths you pave. No words are equal
to your true and just praise. Baptize me, make me for once true and
complete. My logic is shallow, show me the lost equation for being deep.
I am baffled by you and will always lack the words to define you.
I realize,
I don't need to.

Sleeping Good

I went to sleep last night at ease. No not because the world was without sleaze, or there were no hungry families. I went to sleep and I dreamed of platinum bling, of R&B singers half dressed and shaking they thing. I dreamed of Bentleys, ultra thin phones, and rap cats ripping microphones. With Dolce in the panties and a 44 magnum on their waists, mean grills on their face. Oh yes, I slept good last night because my 10 gallon hat stood so high and a pair of tight expensive jeans wrapped my thighs, not because the world was made better.

Sleeping good, damn good.

Last night before I slept I indulged in steak and fine cuisines. I stuffed my face. My Nikes tied tightly, bagging on those with pants sagging how they carry and sell drugs, but we should be better and show them love. Did their mamas not give them hugs? Were they raised like little brown bugs, learning nothing but to be filled with uselessness? What more do I need to give? Yes my Benz will be filled with the blood of the Middle East, my diamonds the blood of Africans, my leather and furs, animals on the verge of extinction, but I will sleep good.

I will sleep damn good.

As he slept, into his room crept the poet scientist, the wordologist to speak a forgotten, misused phrase in his ear. When he wakes he will wake with a tear and without fear, this is what it said...

The struggle isn't dead!

Revolution is what it is called for the sake of those to fall I will call it evolution. They wince at the hint of blood shed in public beds, doing their dirt in secret instead. Man, woman the struggle is not dead, just a little weak. Suffering from atrophy, spina bifida, or maybe iron deficiency, but not lacking in the coefficient.

Sleeping Good

Man, woman heed the omen. The struggle has never been about color. "Brother" is all men, even those who would stab me for my goods, those who would throw drugs in condemned hoods. Human rights are not black or white, but human, mortal flesh and bones. We all die with words on tombstones, yet you have the nerve to serve up the same thing dealt to you, to discriminate and indulge and give the same hate that was given to you. Put in your blood instead.

I repeat for the hearing dysfunctional the struggle is not dead!

It is alive on Crenshaw, on Slauson, in Baldwin, in Miami, in Tuskegee, up North and everywhere you look someone's getting shook. Someone's being tricked, dicked and fucked not licked and stuck, with no attempt at smoothing the act of them being pimped. Like chimps we do our master's bidding, forgetting what we are here for. No, the struggle isn't dead just got locked up in Compton with a couple of dumb kids. No, the struggle isn't dead it's in hiding like Elvis. No man, the struggle is not dead it's just hiding from the man. Apparently the struggle has been considered a menace to society for evading taxes. I ask this then, where is the struggle? And I answer from Beverly Hills to the slums of New York from Compton to wherever human rights are violated. Human rights are not black or white but human.

That night he did not sleep good. He woke with tearing eyes that had found a real reason to cry, an angered heart that had found a reason to die.

He didn't sleep good.

March

The African drums, low with the voice of the feminine hum, like hips being swung.
These historical memorials, tutorials, words that few have heard,
from her lips to his nerve, provoking movement so swift it is beyond your curve.

This is the song of the past, amassed. The foundation of the future itching the skin of the sovereign like grass. They are so crass, without benefit of thought or class. More concerned with the size of her ass, and if at last she will give them that pussy pass, that for days they have asked.

What have we marched for, so that our families would choose to sell heroine to the poor?
That our brothers die overseas and in this domestic war?
All this at the hands of condition ethnicism!
There is only one race.
But they are skilled at throwing mace in the faces of the lost ones.
Trained to inflict physical pain, this, the last thought to be restrained.

March

I mean they all look the same, so why not give them similar names?
What have we marched for?
We have taught ourselves their religions, now we keep ourselves in their prisons.
Tell me will someone listen?
It's not done till it is done.
Till every color white, every color black, every color brown, is given the respect it deserves, or until above all things life is preserved.
Wishful are these words.
What have we marched for? I write this without grief for there is life in the ghetto.
There are doctors in the ghetto, not just prostitutes, drug dealers and hot metal.
There are lawyers in the ghetto.
There is love in the ghetto.
There is heart in the ghetto.
There are not just big booties and babies in the ghetto. There is talent beyond writing, reading and playing sports in the ghetto.
But what do you see in the ghetto? What have we marched for?

No Words

The world was built on pain,

built on those who refuse to use their brains,

built on those who blame everyone else for their short comings and loss of self love. Their ability to open up. Their lack of put up or shut up. So broken and corrupt, the world is filled with he hurt mes, and she hurt mes, and I want to be frees. Like germs it spreads freely. The world is filled with he isn't a man, she isn't a woman but where's the difference? That love and essence, that I don't want to be stressing, the I refuse to be guessing, the I'm tired of second best. That I'm tired of never getting to rest, the I hate to think of less, that I won't stop till I reach heaven's top, that I am someone, that you are someone, even when your actions may appear to be dumb, you are not. Where is that I refuse to be bitter, that they hurt me but I am not a damn quitter, that I will not be hindered, the to pain I will not surrender, that to the right ones I'll be tender, that I will love my gender, that heartless need to be freed, that whoever I choose to fuck me will please, or best believe I will leave? Because the world is filled with heavy hearts that are broken, and once shattered like glass no matter how good the stroking will never be open. But still where are those hoping for something so hot their flesh is smoking? The world is filled with hate provoking, so many lies their intestines are broken. But the world has that already. It already has low self esteem, low tolerance and dreams, people who use and people who are only turned on by abuse. I ask you, when will you be different? These fathers that are bitter raising sons the same, these shitty women raising daughters to be the same, I ask you when are we different? Or are we hell bent on acting indecent towards those who represent difference? I ask you when do we do better? Because the world is filled with people who say so much that we are backed up like a toilet that can no longer flush, I hope the ignorant have heard.

No more words!

Smile

When the world gets you down
it's like everybody wants to fuck you around,
Smile.
When nobody is there when you need them
but got their hands out for you to feed them,
Smile.
I know shit is hard I know it's fucked up
you make the world smile even when your lucks up,
Smile.
Don't let those hataz, procrastinators, weigh you down, you got love all around you, and I'm so glad I found you!
Smile. Oh! You need a reason to smile? Ok, then look at your picture, look at my picture, kiss your daughter. You make me smile every day. Call me when you need me and it won't cost a damn thing, except a smile.
Queen, you bring me joy and that's just with your voice. You inspire me to live and choose the road of choice. I am here for you tell me what you need me to do, Naw! I'm not trying to buy you, I want to hear your smile come through.
Smile.
Smile for your baby girl who brings joy to the world. I know it's hard dealing with them retards. I can't imagine what you go through, everybody trying to fuck you, cause you're so beautiful. You're just trying to make it in this world, but listen baby girl, what you got here is more than sex from me, what you got here is far more than your booty. What you got here is something so deep it will split your hardship in half, if you just let me.

No matter how hard it is or pissed off you are....

Remember to Smile!

Afros and Poetry and Pumping Fists

She arrived at my heart with a brown afro, a caramel glow and a red shirt to accent her red skin. So hurt, but where she had been she did not say, she just spoke out her pain in poetic frames. Written on my heart though she knew not my name, she mastered the art and bypassed the game. She spoke of the hurt and faced her shame.

Afros and poetry and pumping fists!

They pretended to snicker and laugh at her fro. She smiled with red skin and out shined their small flow. It was hate you know, but she blazed on the world with a face that made me smile. She had an attitude of you'd better move but damn I liked her style. She would talk to her heart trying to make her life go with ease. She had men at her beck and call to do what she pleased. But she chose one.

Afros and poetry and pumping fists!

Afros and Poetry and Pumping Fists

She told me things were changing, her life was rearranging. Somehow life had become insane, she was all grown up and it was a constant rain down on her lips. I noticed red skin stained with the wet of hurt and disappointment. She was still trying to get what the point was, trying to make a way for her love, baby and family to live. Damn, she thought something has got to give.

Afros and poetry and pumping fists!

So I saw the pain though she tried to smile. I spoke with my fingertips to the soul child. "Baby do you, when the world gets you down, and makes your caramel face frown. Throw that sad down and do you, because every time you smile the world turns a little faster, the sun shines a little brighter, and I become a better writer."

For you, afros and poetry and pumping fists, much love from the heart. From the head, written with fingertips moved by black wrists for you to stay true.

Unto Herself

She is a universe unto herself, the picture of love and health. She moved her family across roads and country for their safety, never caught in a blur, or thought of what was good for her. She has sacrificed so much and gained so little. She has moved mountain tops and created life from my precious drops. She is without a doubt a world unto a child born through her womb. While men claim the sun she is the universe shining on earth like the moon. She is the mathematical equation, a logarithm of unknown sum, she is one unto herself!

I can write as much as my hand can muster, her luster for life is a window. What she does for her child no one will really know. How she moves this world defying the gravity. She chooses flight, she said it feels so right. She is love unto herself, a compound word of infinite meaning and yet she is so easily understood. If you listen to her heart, her soul, her mind, she will let you know when it is time. She is a blur of beauty, impossible to define. She is the equation that is logic beyond logic, the variant in life unto herself!

There is nothing beyond her focus, her grasp, she can make last look like first when in truth it is their last. If she is consequence then punish me. Let me bask in her energy. She is the equation's answer, the complexity of the science neither condition nor unconditional. She is all these things. She is culture, no specific one, but all of the short and tall of them. From Egypt to Jamaica to the Brazils, Puerto Ricos, Armenias, to the Spains and the Euros she is one unto herself!

Not to every woman, just to the outstanding women!

Bring Your Heart to Me

Miss chocolate bottom, caramel top damn you are so hot, you have caused global warming without any warning. You are not just fine, you are a miracle mind. You stand outside of time and look at how your hips wind. You are the wine of Asia and Africa, now Americanized, but still beating the drum of Africa with each thrust of your thighs. Yeah, they act like they don't know claiming you are dancing like a hoe, call you slut, bitch, porno to video. Oh no, let me educate their hating lips. The way she throws her hips, that's Africa, the way she throws her hips, that's Brazil, the way she shakes her hips, that's Cuba baby. The way she drives men crazy, that's our culture don't be shady. Man, from the pole to the soul she conveys when she speaks from the lust, to the love to the freak, that's the culture baby, that's what drives them crazy.

Listen, they try to put you down because your dress is too short. They call you hoochie because you are proud of the booty. But who are they to judge? What's the reason for their grudge? I mean hate is hate and they don't have no type of love. Man listen, is it the way she shakes her hips like a California tremor? No that's Mexico, el Salvador, Puerto Rico, what are you hating for? Is it the way she twists her hair? No that's the culture. Is it the color in her skin that got you all twisted in a knot or the fact she owns the attention of all men that makes you want to plot? Man that's the culture. Not all of it, a small part of it, and you got to love it, you got to want to lick it and hug it, that's the culture.

Now everybody got disrespect about how she should not be so priceless. I mean she isn't the whole culture, just a small part. So what if she wants to show off the booty, that don't make her a bitch, a hoe, a slut. That makes you a hater, hating on the butt…but she gone keep doing her thang, making rappers and singers sang. Artists will write poems and sonatas about her dundadda and she will be praised for the movement of her hips, she will be adored for the way she moves her lips from the Aztec ruins as far as Africa.

Don't Let it Get You Down

Baby the struggle still leads on. Sometimes I can't see past that chocolate skin, beautiful grin to the pain that's skin deep but resonates without and within. Sometimes my urge to want to hold you out weighs my sense of your true need to be heard, not to be seen as just some physical thing for my greed,

Don't let it get you down.

Baby because I've been watching too many videos and your shape and demeanor so lovely, I focus on sexing you until I make you mine. I day dream of how you wind your hips and lick your lips and take small sips of whatever you are drinking. The sex appeal drips from your aura. I may be selfish trying so hard to get up in it but you just remember

Don't let it get you down.

Baby the struggle is forever lost. I forever pay the cost thinking cash is the way to your ass. You are no man's bitch, no video's hoe, you are no porno's slut, just cause you are blessed with sexiness and know how to shake your butt.

Don't let it get you down.

Don't Let it Get You Down

Baby forgive me for all the times you tried to speak your mind but I was too caught up on your lips to take the kiss from your mind, too caught up in your face to see the hurt in your eyes, busy holding myself trying to get between your thighs, when all you needed was a friend and so your eyes still cry,

Don't let it get you down.

Forgive me for the sexual jokes that broke while you spoke of a hurt that choked so much it cut off your air.
Despair.

Forgive my insecurities, when all you've shown is love to me, in return I act cool as if in the presence of you, you mean nothing to me.

Don't let it get you down.

Forgive me, even now instead of just saying forgive me for being a selfish, sexist, insecure, unsure of himself pig, I make it pretty. You have to understand, I seek so hard to impress you, even in my need to undress you. Truth is you inspire me to be more than free, I worship and thank you.

To all my sisters.

Don't let it get you down.

Afros, Dreads, Nappy, Bald Heads

She wears a crown in the form of an afro,
she lets it blow in the wind, again and again.
I say, "Damn! Why does she not turn my way?"
Why can't she turn left at the Niles of Africa?
Down in the stream the fish laugh at the way I stare at her sway,
when she garlands my way.

She is apple fresh, sweetened with whipped topping.
She is sweet chocolate rain dropping on my tongue.
Her nappy natural so full and all, making her stand so proud and tall,
yet for a peasant she is so much like Fall…

Winter…
Spring…
Summer…

Ever changing, her life rearranging like afros, dreads, nappy, bald heads!
She is synonymous with African wear like bed sheets on skin so bare.
She is an intrusion.
The bald head she wears proudly declares,
"Fuck you, I am beautiful regardless of my hair!"
Expressions so truthful.
She walks with the wind,
her hips entrance me again and again.

Afros, Dreads, Nappy, Bald Heads

She is never outdated.
Like Angela Davis unoppressed and so hated.
I stand by the pyramids for years and wait.
She is a fantasy I anticipate.

For so long like a Stevie Wonder song I await
her arrival, it helps in my survival.
Just to see her revival, afros, dreads, nappy, bald heads!

Her dread locks are chocolate strands
of her heritage wrapped in her headband.
It is like the perfect marriage of color to the eyes of all brothers.
She is adored as a friend, leader, lover and mother.

She is a gift from so high that even I do not speak its name.
She is an anomaly, unnatural yet oh so natural.
With her natural do, however truth be due, she is taken by you know who.
He must be a heavenly body to attract somebody like her.

As I stand by the under current of her funk, I hope to hear her say, "I love you," a dream I fear will never come true. Sporting afros, dreads, nappy, bald heads!

In a Moment

Somewhere along the edge of honesty and the back of trust,
running from the tribe of love and falling off the cliff of lust
I asked her, "Are you lost for what you don't have, and if you did have what you don't have,
would you want more?" She replied, "You are a word whore."
"Not as much a word whore as you are for attention.
Also did I mention you look like roses and chocolate?
You smell and taste so sweet, when you are next to me."
She understood that I wanted all the goods.
She was willing to express her feelings,
so we went back to Crenshaw. Damn she was sorely needed.

And in a moment…

There was peace, a brief stillness, for once no drive bys, no tears in mother's eyes.
Brothers stared as we walked hand in hand, there was no disrespect, no grabbing their dicks,
just love and admiration for who I came with.
"Oh, by the way, what be's your name?" She smiled a little ashamed and so sweetly her words
came, "I was known as Cleopatra a few thousand years before a tragic end brought me to tears
and more. Also in my former life I was a poet extraordinaire they used to call me Gwendolyn
Brooks my name was in all the history books."

And in a moment...

In a Moment

He came with a ride and fame, a pimp with such game that he put even truth to shame.
He walked past me. She noticed his flossing and showed not a hint of atrocity. But when I turned, my heart burned for she was no longer there.
From bald head, to afro she didn't stop. Dashikis and dreaded locks she was still hot.
But one day, out of nowhere she permed her hair, and walked about without a care.
African blood diamonds on her neck and a nine in case a n*&^@ disrespect, she called her self that bitch, hood rat and shit.
No longer did she pump the black fist instead she sold her ass for tricks and I think she's anti-dick.

And in a moment...

Nothing has changed much, though the struggle slowed down, we still keep in touch.
I used to write my heart out the best way I could, telling her how much I loved her though
In a moment….
she's lost in the hood.

Baby Do You

Listen girl in this crazy world of
sexism, pseudo realism,
off the wall things, that make your ears ring,
no matter who you talk to
make sure you do you.
Because we all have our issues,
sometimes we will misuse.
Hell that's the issue.
Black girl, brown girl just do you,
no matter what they say
smile, throw your hips, walk away.
No matter how they sneer,
walk these streets with no fear.
Listen dear! Do you baby.
If you think red is green, black is blue,
if you think the sky is filled with diamonds
for no one but you,

Baby Do You

if the entire world stands against you and sends mockery you stay true to you. Baby do what you do.
When your man gets you down,
all those you love are nowhere to be found,
stand on your own two.
You are more than beautiful,
more than sexy,
more than chocolate skin.
You are no ones woman but your own.
Baby read the omens and leave them haters alone.
Baby do you.
If the world can't see what you are truly capable of
then tell them to kiss the dirt because hate will get no love.
You are Venus, Mars, all the universe's stars. You are spirit, church all the things that work. You are infinitely wise and more than just the heaven between your thighs. You are you, that is more than any being will ever be able to say of you, or do for you.

Stand firm.

True baby do you!

Caught

I am caught between her breast and the struggle of stress. Yes, I am caught between wanting her and wanting to forget her. I am wishing in my mind to make her a blur. I am caught between the slave trade and the road unpaved. In fact I am stranded on the road unmade. She has me on rocks and sand with my heart for her in my left hand…caught.

I am caught between her chocolate mind, kiss and behind. Just because she is dark don't mean she's the one. Just because her hips move the sun don't mean she needs to have my son but I am lost in the sweet movement of her dance. I pray for only the chance to love her like no other, to be that brother, the one who wants to be smothered with her love...caught.

I am in love with her attitude she is so damn rude. How she gets what she wants and how she flaunts and taunts. How at times she is so humble lifting you when you stumble. The right woman will never let you crumble even when your ego makes you fumble. She is the bee, honey sweet, the butterfly, a floating reflection in the iris of my eye. I am completely and utterly in her presence even when she's gone…caught.

Stolen

I kneeled to worship her shackled feet. She turned away in disgust of me. I prayed to gods during the Egyptian age, and walked with Martin for her love to be saved. Yet, she still turned away from me. Like gazelles from predators she tended to flee, during the time she was taken from her history.

Stolen....

Maybe I did not deserve her grace. I have felt the lost honor of not being the center of her heart's attention. See if I could not protect her, if I could not keep her from that slave trade those whites made Swahili from I deserved her love none. I rested at the moon of her ass still on my way to her heart at last. I just hoped one day she would see through the gray.

Stolen....

I loved her essence though I was taught to focus on her shape. I loved her arrogance though we were raised with the minds of over-sexed apes. She was my culture or that which would be its representation and without her love I was lost in lack of verbalization. What was I to say? Nothing, she had been sold and her family taken away.

Stolen....

This is an old tale of an ancient hell. I was lost without her love, lust, touch, fuck, anger, guidance and direction. She was the sole reason for my erection. With her I was Darwinist for she was my natural selection.

Stolen....

I found myself at the peak of her breast. She had by then removed her dress to feed her family and relieve her stress. She shook her hips in strip clubs for tips, on videos and shit, and I watched her every bit. Not to berate her no part of me could ever hate her. Yet in my mind it was the only way to be with her, to let her know that I would never forget her. Hoping she would see that without her affection, attention, my life was a blur.

Stolen....

Change the World

She came with chocolate, diamond nipples singing African tunes.
She swayed her hips to the beat of the drums and shined in the night moon.
I was lost like African tribes in the desert with no nourishment.
Then I saw her mirage and all the love that her heart sent.
She rode the land she never walked always ran with love in her heart
and fresh water in her hand.
She took me in caressing my stressed heart,
whispering in my ear that we would never be apart.
I was found in the Mohaves and Saharas cooking in the heat.
She gave me a smile that alone took away the weight from my feet.
I now live in fun never do I walk I always run,
with love in my heart and her with my son.
We came with chocolate, diamond nipples,
butterflies sending out an effect in ripples.
We are changing the world.

Timeless Love

He is the prince one day soon to be king embodying all things masculine, loving to his women who fantasize about his chocolate skin. He is the protector being held in his arms is to be ushered away from all harm. His softness is strength in the wake of his dense, sense of love for his culture, his wife, his girl, his mama, his sister, the woman who cares for him. She is amazed at how he wears his clothes. He stands to the side to hold the door, a gentle man, with chocolate covered skin. He is sexual for her or him, he is sensual for them, he is drenched in the lust of Africa.

His arms are comfort to her soft skin. Nostalgia is the reccurring smell of him. They are at a loss for words, when his manhood touches their nerves. All of their screams are heard clear when his love is given, what they deserve. He is a teacher, poet, mathematician, scientist of the heart and the mind. He is so fine, with a love outside the laws of time.

He is the father, son, love untouched and not compared to anyone. He is the caramel candy that makes life sweet. He is a plethora of knowledge, a book of sensual healing, exposing his heart to them. They are in his line of sight but to them he is blur. He could move mountains with his love for them. He is a statue, statuesque like a monolith. They adore his attitude, the mojo he exudes.

He is for them a timeless love.

Broken Heart

It has been stabbed, kicked, punched, licked, yet
it still ticks. Keep on keeping on got to stay strong,
can't lose my will to love,
my will to hold can't become stone,
then something's wrong.
Life I ask you to please inspire me to unbound heights.
Give me the strength to love like no man and enjoy the hurt.

Take away my broken heart.

Universe I ask you to give me the freedom to love with out hindrance to touch without inhibition, to kiss with no restriction, to hold with no hate, to release all things and their weight.

It's been kicked, cut, shot, stabbed, but please I ask you broken heart don't die. Stay with me so that I can mend you, change and transcend you, flex your hardness so that I can bend you to my will to love.

Let me mend you broken heart.

Insanity

He speaks in uncontrolled moans and tweaks. He is labeled a freak.

His tone is spoken deep, low. Insanity? Or does he realize what we don't know?

Salt and pepper hair, peanut butter brown skin and a blue duffle bag with a tear on the end. Insanity. He stands, back pressed against inner indifference hence a hint of his minds power spent. Years far from the norm, was this the way he was born? Having no hold on our reality or are we the lost and he the found? Is he trying to show us the way through incoherent sounds? Insanity? Is he a prophet with his hand pressed to the side of his head, trying to warn us of the road down which we have been led? Insanity. For a second I am too deep in my own awaking sleep to even peep his mental retreat. I am the lost one, the caught one in this web spun. Is he still overcooked like vegetables and raw like meat 'til we are over done?

Insanity.

Forsaken

He drove Cadillacs as he improved his mack, only to find out the hard way even with money like Donald Trump he is still black. Still, he waited by the words of lost pimps trying to find his mojo. He stood on the corners by schools trying to find a new hoe. His legs began to tire as he searched in vain for a status much higher. He reached to the sky with elastic out stretched arms filled with gold and platinum charms. He tried to get as close to God as he could with ass, money and any drug that was good. He sang, danced and wore the paint of chance, expensive cologne but he was just trying to get home. Trying his best to avoid arrest and white men with ropes using hate to give the poor hope. He wrote lyrics with an unknown form dictating how he would never conform, while at the same time narrowing his vision becoming more like those who had once imprisoned...him. Now after all these years she is a bitch to him. Completely smoked out and further out on a limb, he is no longer unique, no longer strong he is weak. His only defense on these streets is being tense and a gun on his hip for those like him with no sense.

Blue Tarp

Maybe it will keep the rain out. I think religious hymns are what her throat sang out. She sat on the cold concrete with water splashing at her feet. She yelled in words that could not be comprehended, asking for assistance, going to late night restaurants for bathrooms to piss in. Blue tarp, it may keep the rain away, it may hide the pain today, but will she use it tomorrow and if not will it take away her sorrow?

She wore a tainted, dirty, painted wedding dress. In her mind wearing the garment she looked her best. But who will she marry? Who will take her hand and carry her to the Promised Land? What person will wed her heart? What beautiful soul will honeymoon her away from this homeless decay? Or kiss her swollen, bruised feet and see the beauty beneath? How much louder must she sing before we acknowledge her existing?

Do we need to be two checks away from poverty, just to see how easily we can be filthy and smelling like pee? What do we need to understand this misery? The cart she pushes or maybe the cart that pulls her along, maybe that is who she's talking to trying to figure out exactly what went wrong. The bitter cold rolls in and still to the bars of her cart she is holding. What from her mind, soul or heart was stolen?

What was taken for her life to be frozen? Now she wears the same clothing and everyday the same words are spoken, "Someone see me! Help me! Free me!" But her blue tarp speaks no pain, it only blocks the rain.

Ode to the Streets

This is my ode to the streets.
This is my song to all those who have no place to sleep.
My symphony to the bum with no shoes on his feet,
my untamed beat.
Like roaches and rats and rainy weather that makes flesh stink,
this is for the depraved and deprived,
on every corner there's a church but for all God don't provide.
This is for the pee smelling,
on the corner dwelling,
mind been gone,
from whatever drug they was on,
street felon.
These words for prostitutes with crack in their nerves,
flesh wrinkled body tainted,
but she still on the corner face painted,
selling herself cheap.
This is my ode to the streets.
This is my sonnet to the mindless,
homeless,
foodless,
eaten up by stress.

Ode to the Streets

Deteriorating to the point where they're foolish,
these streets got them clueless.
And me and you we don't do shit,
but continue to pass by and spit,
comments,
so horrific,
like they want to be starving,
freezing,
selling their bodies to keep eating,
walking all night to keep from sleeping,
done cried so much they all dried up so no more
weeping.

Dementia.

They slip deeper and deeper into a different zone,
now they only speak to no one man their minds gone,
this is my song,
to true poverty where there's nothing to struggle for,
'cause they don't want to try no more,
the hurts too deep.

Ode to the Streets

This is my ode to the streets.
This is my one man play,
of dreams deferred and smoked away,
or shot up veins,
to eradicate someone's pain,
but it never works,
the drugs never kill the hurt,
it's like a baby blanket trying to cover the earth.
This is my sitcom to the family living in a car,
pissing in an old water jar,
living short and dreaming far,
hoping for better,
while chasing dreams of cheddar.
This is my soliloquy to those who push a buggy,
begging for change if they get a dollar they're feeling
lucky. Carrying covers,
do they think about their dead mothers,
or does the smell of decay,
take the past away?
Damn I know they can't wait to get off their feet,
so this is for them, my ode to the streets.

Let Me Paint

She came to me in the dawn of the sun falling…saying, "Let me paint my sex all over your flesh. Let my tongue be the brush stroke to make you erect. Let me paint on your heart the desire to protect. Let me paint my sexy all over your flesh. Let me paint...." She came to me in the early dawn, never giving me a chance to yawn. Her kiss on my lips the equivalent of the first atomic bomb. Her intention to make my extension her own, she wanted me in ecstasy for the long term. She said, "Let me paint my love all over your blank heart. Let me paint my love with my hands. Let me paint...."

She came to me after the rooster's crow with chocolate caramel skin that I adored. She looked like a goddess in her earth tone dress, all I knew was her flesh I longed to caress. "Let me paint my lust on your skin. Let my strokes paint on your face ecstasy when your body is holding me. Let me paint something so deep in your soul, you could dig for eternity and never reach its goal. Let me paint...."

"Let me paint this love potion all over your swaying motion, tears in your eyes not from pain of any kind, but from physical explosions. Let me paint the perfect distraction and me the only thing on your mind. Let me paint...."

Miss Pretty Feminine

When you are in the room there is sunshine.

Don't let doubt get in your mind.

You are too fine, love that you need is in you indeed,

and you shall succeed,

with lips like candy,

and a soft wool fro.

You know you are a goddess,

at least I hope you know.

The world moves at the twist of your hips.

Men bow when you pucker your lips.

You send out lust from your fingertips.

Smile.

Miss Pretty Feminine

You are the reason we exist

to do silly shit

for your attention to get.

One is so lucky to touch your soft skin.

You are a breeze on a hot day that keeps on blowing.

I am at a loss for words,

nerve,

strength,

in your presence bent.

Miss Pretty Feminine

I wish I was there to argue with you,

say poetry in your ears,

kiss away your caramel and chocolate tears,

but I am in these words,

written to your heart to touch your nerve.

Saying hold on cause what you deserve

is sunshine in the dark,

an always loving heart.

Can I whisper in your ears

thoughts of written sexuality,

alter the way you perceive this reality?

Miss Pretty Feminine

Touch

my

lips

to your

lips

to your

hips

to your

ears

to your

thighs

to your

Miss Pretty Feminine

heart and so deep inside,

to make your eyes cry tears of joy

and scream at the top of heavy lungs oh Boy!

I love you!

Low moans and continuous lusty explosions,

inner implosions

the pain falling away in corrosion.

You are a gift to be cherished

and so should it be

forever in eternity.

My words

my lust

my love

my affection

in the written world

Much written love so that it will never be forgotten!

Squeeze

At some point her voice became soft

I could tell she was wet as hell from getting

Off

It was as if the lubrication between her

Thighs

Was making it easy to move through life

Squeeze

She obeyed each command

Spoken from her chosen man

Squeeze

I love you barely breaking from her lips

The ideas being expressed from her hips

Squeeze

Squeeze

The heavy breathing from her muscle

Squeezing

As if I were mentally teasing

Her soul

Squeeze

Her breath erratic ecstasy

Breaking from her allowing me

Control of her body

Squeeze

At many different points the smoothness in

Her voice

Gave me insight into how much she was

Moist

Squeeze

Foundation

Allow me to lay rose petals at your feet, my heart given and it's for keeps. Let me give you bubble baths in the wake of the days dying aftermath. Naked flesh blazes our paths. Express your screams of passion and wrath, allow my mind to express itself too. Allow my body to get so close to you that now there's one when there were two. It would feel like…Coconut milk baths that make your face grin, my lips on your clit, my tongue is the key let me in!

Allow me to massage the tension from the small of your back, magic fingers attack, I know you'll love that. Allow me access to your treasure chest, your precious jewels, your love nest, trust me I'll do the rest. Now the ride may start bumpy but in the end you will be cumming, feels beyond stunning. When tears start running down your sweet soft cheeks, it would be like…Coconut milk baths that make your face grin, my lips on your clit, my tongue is the key let me in!

Allow me to make your mind explore all physical possibilities. Your back your thighs, your lips, your eyes all focused on me. Let me bring not sexy back, but sex back. To the side, from the back, long deep strokes what your body lacks. Allow me to caress your waist as my lips touch your face. You can't breathe, you can scream, bitten lips like cold ice cream. Let me take you to that dream. It would be like…Coconut milk baths that make your face grin, my lips on your clit, my tongue is the key let me in!

Allow me to paint ecstasy on the flesh I see. Allow me to give you the tools to trust. I know you've been through a lot but everybody needs to explode in lust. Let me take you beyond orgasm, continuous physical spasms. As I taste your skin I'll be so deep your head will spin, your back will bend. You will hold me like a dying man holding on to dear life, and I will not let you down. I will always please my wife. It would be like…Coconut milk baths that make your face grin, my lips on your clit, my tongue is the key let me in!

My Friend

There she is with the sway in her hips, with those dark chocolate lips. She doesn't need your war paint she is beauty. She defies all logic, she is logic so deep. She moves more than my soul, more than my groin. She moves my universe, she is my essence. I want to be made her essence. She moves my ground, I am unstable in her grasp. I am lost at last. I am in a frenzy, dizzy, waiting on her call. I have fallen so deep in you. I feel so next to you, my friend, my sexy, mama, queen, let me taste Africa once before I die. Allow me passage to your wet Nile. Allow me to be so close to your rain forest as to taste your cool dew. Allow me the permission to engulf your lips, to taste your tongue. Freely I will give all, is that to much? I will give more if all is not enough. My friend, my sexy mama, queen, goddess see my beauty as I see yours, as a pool of cool that I must drown in.

I Look Into Your Eyes

I look into your eyes and see
so much pain, so much hurt.
I just want you to know you can count on me.
I want you to know I am here for you.
So whatever you are going through my words will always be true. I look into your eyes and see
disappointment, and I know what to do. I just want you to know I won't disappoint you.
Wherever you tread, I'll be there to pull you through. I look into your eyes and what do I see?
Your potential to save the world.
Listen girl, you can change the world.
I know because seeing your picture changes my world.
I know why you hold your head up so high.
I'll tell you why,
you are a queen in training, with eternity at your feet.
Your heart has the potential to be so sweet, do not bow to defeat. I look into your eyes...
My heart smiles, I am bewildered by you.
I am enthralled in you,
that's why I write these words to you.
If only you knew what my heart says when I see you.
Black queen, ruler of the universe all I ask is this one thing,
see me past your pain,
past the doubt.
I look into your eyes...

Walk to My Door

It was so seductive the constructive way she laid her words at my ear. She spoke like an Aaliyah song begging for my affection to come near. *"Can I come over?"* Damn, I can't help but smile. She's so sexy, so full of charisma and she is asking to be lying on my chest so sexily, playing sweet love songs in the background with nothing on. "You know a house is not a home," she smiled she knew she had it going on. I listened to her explain how my house was closer to her job and how she needed to see me tonight to make every thing alright.

Walk to my door.

She said, "Hold up I got to call you back because of my battery." Those seconds seemed like years damn near bringing me to tears. However, just when I was about to explode the ringing tone from the phone unloads. Her sexy voice is sent to my ears, "Are you there?" As if there is a chance in hell that I would not be.

Walk to my door.

She already knew the answer there was no doubt of her intent, "I'll be there soon," my emotions swirl like a storm of monsoons. I cannot speak, I am always weak in her presence but somehow strong. She's on her way over and though it wont be too long it seems like forever. I call a couple of times just to ease my own mind. I light candles, pour wine, dim lights and curse time. But I won't have to wait a minute more.

Walk to my door.

Something Different

It is a fact that the world turns at whatever speed the universe deems it needs. It is a fact that tradition is the seed that is planted and normality is the word for clone. It is a fact when you're different you walk alone. It is an inevitable law that no matter what your flaw, no matter which you are if you focus on that fleeting star, the universe will answer.

I asked for someone to understand me and I received someone who understands her. I asked for a queen and received a goddess, the hottest sensual, spoken word artist. I asked for peace, I got a vanilla chocolate, sweet mellow, soothing melodic voice oozing, doing things to my body that honestly nobody has accomplished. My only wish is that she was mine. If I told her this she would probably smile and say ever so poetically, 'in time'."

I ask, "Do you understand having ones favorite meal in front of them and not being able to indulge in it? Being so hungry from dissatisfaction and being told, 'in time?' To be a virgin and never have been touched and to finally meet someone that you want to and I make no apologies fuck? To want to taste her body, the first body you have ever seen and wanted to devour and be told, 'in time?' To be thirsty, close to death and for the first time seeing something that your palette and your head and heart and soul wants to take in whole, only to be told 'in time'?"

"To finally taste the spoken words equal to yours in intensity, in complexity, in richness and sincerity. It is a wonder to be spoken to ever so genuinely and so sexily. A knowledge that you have waited to hear from another's lips for so many years, then for that person to be wrapped in your favorite skin. To don your ideal style and you adore my style as well only to be told, 'in time.' To want to squeeze her so tight as to convey, or say in physical actions what no poetic words could even come close to expressing and be told, 'in time'?"

Something Different

"To be completely satisfied when her voice is heard, in other words, I was in no way diminished in the want of hearing her vocalizations. I want more. Wanting to tell her come over now so that I can impress you, and impress upon you all the things I am able to do to you. Bring you tears of joy. My love would be no chains only pleasure, no pain. I will give you ecstasy, physically, mentally, spiritually. But I am told, 'in time'."

To finally see in you difference, from your style to your choice words, from your lips to my heart. I am at a loss for nothing. You inspire me to create beyond all that is before me. You did that before you spoke to me, you inspire me to life. I want to breathe, just to know you and the seed that grows next to you. You are so many things, so far outside the boundaries of even my poetry. I promise even in my frail attempts to describe you I will not confine you.

It is written in books, wisdom in the trees, ask and you shall receive, I have asked and my wish has been freed.

Rain Drops

As the warm rain drops

My head is filled with hot sex thoughts.

Falling, falling, falling, falling,

To my groin.

Day dreams of sexy thighs,

Smiling eyes

That in joy cry, voices that yell so high

Why?

It feels so damn good,

Like nothing you've ever felt if your heart is open

You will want it all for yourself.

Falling rain drops on naked skin

Rolling down on soft chins.

Smiles.

Screams and grins.

Making love with grown and sexy friends.

Rain Drops

I hope these rain drops never end.

Falling,

Moisture,

From between her luscious thighs,

Wildness in her eyes.

Her screams...

Warm, wet.

Love from above that moves to below.

Raindrops of orgasms,

Smashing walls,

Cumin' water falls.

Rain drops.

Rolling down my skin pops my senses back to what I lack,

To the drops I catch.

Raindrops fill my head like hot sex thoughts,

Sexy thighs and crying eyes.

Rain drops.

Thoughts, Words, Touch

I count the minutes until I hear her words, maybe a little to soon for her to know these words, but if I must be honest, and I must be me, then these words must say where my soul wants to be. She is chocolate cake, she is sweet to the taste, wanting of a tender touch, when her words first touch me I know this much. I want her, I need to have her, not control her, her freedom is what is so entrancing, got my soul dancing. I am a plethora of romancing, she is in control of my heart, my chest, my arms, my groin. Wishes for her sweet kisses, her lips are…

Thoughts, words, touch.

She is my candlelight vigil, my virility, my fertility, though I have only spoken to her a few times. No, she is not always on my mind she is my mind. Her words, her thoughts so fine a perfect vintage wine with a new twist. Had locks, had knots, loves dreads, adores bald heads. Can I hold you? Can I hold your heart, your hand, your soft sexy, intelligent self? Can I hold your entire being in my soul? Pleasing you is my main goal.

Thoughts, words, touch

I Want To

I was trying to find my way back to the diamond mines. That is where I was sent away from her sweet chocolate lips. She is so defined in the written sarcasms of verbs and nouns of the mass burial of the feminine soul. Her lips spit fire as her heart in the form of words leapt from ear to ear. I watched, I felt as they jumped from spirit to spirit asking, "Can you see what is before you and me?" She made no apology for her truths. It was like freedom from the desert of Jews, after forty years of unblessed solitude. At war with those who hate their halves, their sexualities hidden amongst the idea that her breast were not her own. This is the philosophy that her soul was to be owned, and she was never to have a thought erupt from the core of the amygdales. Her thoughts would never course through to her thalamus, to be expressed in the synapse or as a synaptic spark. Never blowing all doubt away. I want to be consumed in the chocolate of her skin. Her words like leprosy infecting me, telling me of the struggle of my skin. She is more than an intriguing venue, she is more than a physical menu. I want to be enthralled in you, to soak up the knowledge that experience has been through. It is my dream to be caught in her dreads like the deepest thoughts that flow through her head. She is so much more than a soldier, she is a goddess of wordom. I will completely succumb to her essence, which is yet unknown to me. I want to taste of her spirituality, to connect with her mentality, and be drowned in her physicality. I want to know this woman deeply as if scientifically. I want to know her as a fact, unlike a theory or hypothesis. I do exist. Her words fill my soul with a light, a darkness that has been long missed. She is what I have always wanted, dreamed for and thought of. She does not know me. I am the written words in her poetry.

I want to…

What I Feel for You

Afternoons so hot sweat drips down the nape of her neck. She has my attention erect. Cold, she eases my need, my greed, my over obsession with her sexiness. She is a storm in my world, a tsunami to my small beating heart. She has had me so high that the sky was a million miles below. When she speaks her tongue is like a million poets. I am amazed at her flow. She is the lost tribes of Africa. The heart of European culture, she is the Asia Minor of soul. She is the essence of butterflies… beautiful not realizing the power of just flapping their wings. She throws her hips and does the same thing.

What I feel for you.

My dream, my reason for doing these things, my written word, my only nerve I feel through you. For you are my change in mood, my mode, my soul and spirit, my essence. Do you hear it the pound of my physical heart? You are the perfectly aimed dart missing only that which does not matter. You are my pain, torn away like mad lovers taking the wall of clothing from their skin. Every reason I breathe, the reason I write these deeds all for you. If you did not exist I would not exist. You are my Christmas, my religion. Yes, I am lost in your intrigue, you are the only book I will ever read.

What I feel for you.

Eyes, Soul, Loss of Control

Her eyes made the dry lands wet with tears, they obliterated the insecurities and fears of men worldwide. Her passion was seen so clear, so easily she has given all her secrets and regrets. Like the swift tongue she throws out words all in honesty, revolution, revelation wanting depth of relationships. See her light eyes through the rain of her emotion soothing the dry seas of my soul, my heart beat pounds, my emotions accelerate, succumbing. She is a beast of beauty, she is so honest, so cunning. Why is she there and not here? Why am I here and not there? The stir of emotion echoes like a dark stairwell that seems empty only to eyes that cannot see the depth of the dark there. Whispered in her ears, sex, love, lust in her eyes, you are magic. My words are erratic, emotion soft on hard skin like lotion, changing her disposition. Please listen, the sight of you is a glimpse into heaven, far from the ghetto to the suburbs. You are fresh air in the pollution of my life and that's just from sight not even written words caught leaving my fingertips. I imagine dancing and her smiling chocolate lips slightly, caramel hips that whip in a fashion not of sex but joy at the music of a band that has her attention. I wish I was that song, that music, the beat that she rides so sweet. She makes the crowd move even more beautifully, so seductively, so free. Such a queen or dare I say a sight of God to me? It is what it is eyes, soul, loss of control.

Strawberries, Whipped Cream, Chocolate Ice Cream

Climax

Like strawberries, whipped cream, chocolate ice cream with me in between, she melts on me. I feel her touch increase in strength and what was meant to be a shock to reality, biting lips and holding hips so tight that marks are left on skin so nice. She breaks down physically over and over, she melts down mentally over and over. There is no rest for her. She is so sweet in her outcry of pleasure, unmeasured, untouched, and yet I am in touch with her soul, in touch with her skin, each push of ecstasy puts me deeper in. She holds me closer and yet her grip melts against my warm chocolate skin like strawberries, whipped cream, chocolate ice cream.

Her head is dizzy with ideas and none of them make sense. Her breath is rapid on my neck, her moans and screams so intense. She scratches my back but no pain is sensed, for there is no pain in dessert. Ice cream may be cold but it will only melt, once hot skin is felt. She buries her face in my neck to smell my sweat and to control her release. As she melts so freely all around me there is no stopping. I will never be done, my only goal in this world is to make her soul cum and run as she melts like, strawberries, whipped cream, chocolate ice cream.

Her explosions are violent. Each one so close to the first one until there is no separation, just one long fat one. Continuous, strenuous, this is us in love, like and lust. Her stomach tightens, her thighs are boa constrictors around my waist, there is only the sight of ecstasy on her face. Her mind is a whirlwind, a tsunami to her soul, she is in a vortex and losing all control of her strawberries, whipped cream, chocolate ice cream.

And I thank the universe this is no dream.

Dick Addiction

She sat with her legs crossed as I mentally took her clothes off.
She was wet before my tongue and her clit ever met.
Her beautiful flesh was tantalized before I even parted her soft thighs.
She spoke of her pussy power how it gushed with sweet hotness for hours and hours.
All I could do is smile as she said, "Listen chil' I can make your toes curl, I can make your mind swirl!"
She spoke of how she tastes so sweet and how I would be addicted to her.
Well at that point, I stopped her flow with a tongue that licked her slow.
Me, I am never harassing the clit just saying hello with a kiss and moving quick to the slit.
Her knees buckled. Her back bent. Her tone changed, her voice sang higher than Aretha Franklin when she sings those notes. I smiled as lust touched her lips and jumped from her sexy ass throat.
I was done talking. I inserted ex amount of chocolate pleasure stretching her walls beyond her mental measure. She clawed at my back and like the hammer from a gun my thighs slid back. She prepared herself for deeper impact gushing cum. I had to hold her she tried so hard to run. Mama's head started to spin, she was in heaven, hell, as I swelled so deep in. As we fucked she lost all control of her soul. Her body failed her and began to leak without control…for me.

Dick Addiction

I pushed to the left and then softly to the right. Swirling my mixer in her tight bowl she was high in lust's flight. Remembering all those spoken words of how she could make me her nerd. Of how she would make me an addict to the pussy, now she was an addict to me. See, I would not stop even when she was completely exhausted my hips continued to pop. Though oxygen was for her rare and hard to get in her lungs, with her legs on my shoulders she continued to cum, and cum and cum and cum. Then finally each cum connected and became one cum continuously it came and continuously she called my name. She spills her soul as she lost all inhibition and shame. Damn she came and I was solely to blame. Yet I still did not stop as my hips continued to pop her lower lips continued to drop… cum.

She is now and forever captivated never speaking again of the power of the p. She only speaks in loud screams when dealing with me. It was taken to the limit, 12 hours and at the end of the flight, I guess she did have some power because I made her fine ass my wife.

Let Me Write You Happy

Love, if just for a second close your burning eyes and as you plummet before you hit the ground I will replace your plunge with rise.

I will replace the tears in your multicolored eyes with rise. At your worse when your soul is down, I will write in place of your hurt a smile.

Shut your eyes tight and let all your doubt go away like last night let it be a distant dream an intangible thing.

Is that just a memory? Let me change that broke to rich then that dead to alive and awoke. Let me change that rape to love found not too late.

Let me write your rage into love beyond this page. Let me write your homeless heart free and secure.

Let me write your deepest desires even if they are not for me. Let me devour your hurt and defecate profound happiness beyond that shut gate.

Let me write you happy.

I Want to Know You

She presented her likes and dislikes and I asked if I was just right. Would I come on to strong if I spoke to her too long? You see it's one thing to be sexy, it's another thing to be grown. Maybe I'm not being clear, but I'm bidding for your heart dear. Maybe I should send you roses? Or words the golden color of the sun to match your skin? Ok, how do you feel about chocolate Miss sexy? By that I mean do you like chocolate lips, are they sweet to your creamy hips?

I want to know you.

Do you ever wonder about chocolate arms keeping you safe from harm?
Or do you dream about coconut milk baths and me working my charm? I am just letting you know that if I saw you on the street, at a show, with your man I would still step to you. Does one pass by a diamond on the street? And since you are more than a diamond where should my mind be? Now hold up, I am not trying to be pushy, wussy, or mushy but I promise you excitement and the attention you deserve. I promise to always keep you curious and to let you know I am serious.

I want to know you.

I Want to Know You

Now when I say, "I want to know you," that means all that encompasses you. Do you want me? Your heart, your soul, in this world your role is this. What do you wish me to know? What do you like about being close? Do you like being close? Are you into romance have you ever been romanced? I can make you smile with a glance. Do my words move your soul? Does your body lose control? Do you want to give me a chance? Now I may not be the one but I am not just anyone, and I promise you what others have failed to do I will get done.

I want to know you.

You've got this whip appeal and damn you look so unreal. Just listen Miss Vanilla, Caramel, Chocolate Rain Drop you already know you're hot. I'm just telling you what I see some soft sexy lips, those beautiful round eyes shining like the moon in a dark room. Intelligence beyond measure, now you need someone to give you pleasure. You need someone to hold you tight and make your heart burst with delight.

I want to know you.

Can't Wait

You left this morning with a kiss and a smile. As you walked past the door you knew I wanted more than that, your smile so truly I adore. As you dressed for your day, I knew that I would be late because I have to watch you move. By the time you've finished, as you walk to the car, me one step close behind you smile and look back. You know you're fine from your hair to your waist line, from your hips to your feet, and you shake more just for me!

I can't wait, I can't wait till you come home, don't be late, don't make me wait too long.

You close the door to your ride, all the while staring in my brown eyes. You roll down your window once again to receive a kiss from your favorite friend. As you pull off you look back, and you look so good when you look back. Almost reminds me when I ride that, when I pull your hair and you arch your back. Now I know I will be late but I just have to wait and see you drive away, can't wait till tonight when you're holding me.

I can't wait, I can't wait till you come home, don't be late, don't make me wait too long.

My boss is all upset but I smile because you I can't forget. Tell him I won't be late again, but in my head I am thinking 'bout my best friend. I was happy when I got your call it made a brother feel extremely tall. You're on my mind like my skull, the way you look, think and all. You tell me how you miss my lips, I close my eyes I can see your hips. Damn, the way you lick your lips, you got a brother trained. Watch me come up with a trick and I know you can't wait.

I can't wait, I can't wait till you come home, don't be late, don't make me wait too long.

Take a Breath

If I breathe you, will you devour my soul?
I want you to.
Will you take a hold and not let go?
I hope you do.
Will you taste my skin, forgive my sins?
I hope you do.
Can you think about me as I do you?
I hope so.
Will you let me love you the way you deserve?
I hope so.
Will you love me the way your heart swerves to?
I hope so.
Will you remain my essence, my cool in a hot breeze?
I hope so.
Damn you're like chocolate radiation look how you glow,
I hope you know how sexy, how beautiful, how much of a queen you are.
You shine for me like a distant star, closer, brighter, stronger. I long for your touch like men long for heaven.
I long for your kiss like a dying man longs for life.
I want to taste your flesh, your soul, your heart.
Be in the midst of your mind, you're so smart.
You are the perfect piece of art, a Mona Lisa to all who see you.
A Monet or sonnet. You are wine for the soul, opening my veins to flow with ease.

Deserve

By all means I did not deserve her kisses. Chocolate luscious lips soft wet to lick. I did not deserve to have been ridden by her wet lust for me. You see I did not deserve the swagger, the swerve, the audacity, the nerve to have her ears even listen to my words. She was lost in the chemical, asymmetrical use of the verbs, the juice that the lips deserve. Yet I did not deserve the sway of her neck so sexy and perfect. And I did not deserve the right to have and hold and all those things yet she is mine.

Deserve.

By all means she did not deserve to even be in my presence. She did not deserve to hear my words spoken in her ear. I am sure I relieve her fear. She did not deserve my unbelievable swirl. She did not deserve my kiss on her neck, my strength and the depth of my stroke. She did not deserve to get her back broke. Truth is she did not deserve to be the honor of my words. She was not even worthy to be romanced in such a way as to push all doubt and keep it at bay. Deserve? She did not deserve my sexiness, my nine inches of thickness. Nor did she deserve my give all regardless love, not a fact never having to act yet she was satisfied.

Deserve.

Who is to say which way should be and which should not? You deserve only what you got, what you chose cons and pros. Do we deserve truth with no doubt for our love not to be used as an excuse for them to break out? Or for them to push their inability to separate sex from love to not believe that the only time one must give their best is in love? She did not deserve and I did not deserve but we got and that is all that matters, for better best or bad worse.

Deserve.

Always On My…

I know I just met you, since we talked I can't forget you. I can't imagine all you go through being a good mother. Though I've never touched you I know you are an amazing lover. Why would you say we've never made love? Baby we have made love, every time I laid you down on my heart. Whenever you let me express my soul to your ears we made love.

I know things may seem hard sometimes. I want you to know 'tho you think we just met you're wrong. I was there every time your daughter showed you she cared. Every time you asked for love I heard, it just took a little time and a little nerve. Every time you touched yourself my tongue tasted your love, I was there. You know me. I am the love that you long for, pure, rich, bitter, sweet, fat, deep. Easy now love…sleep. You know me. I am willing to do all that I can to preserve the strength that is you. I am that listening ear, tell me what you're going through. I want you in my soul, but you're already there.

I want you in my life. I can see you as my wife. I don't want to control you just love you right. I want to move at the speed that's good for you. I want you as my friend. I am willing to hurt for you. I want you to feel safe, completely let me in. When I look at your face I am a newborn my life is about to begin. If it seems I'm moving fast don't worry, just enjoy the ride. It's not that I want you to myself I just got so much love inside. I want you in my head, I want you in my bed, but you already are. I don't know where this will go, but one thing is very clear, you have my heart in your chest and your lips have my ears.

I want you in my...

Diamond

I've tried to be as logical as possible, but she arrives at my nature like wounded soldiers in a hospital. The sound of her giggles y'all, makes my soul tingle, my ball jingle, my mind single out what she's all about.

Damn woman got me rambling, scrambling, stammering for the write or should I say written words to describe her kitten, which is not a kitten at all more like a boa constrictor wrapped around my manhood until I burst in her sweet tight embrace.

More goddess than Aphrodite or she might be more of Isis or Cleopatra, making me want to snatch her from all her woes and sorrows, give her guaranteed sunshine for tomorrow, her souls no longer hollow. She allows me to fill her emptiness, she allows herself to lose control. In her wet African jungle the birth of my child was told.

Wet Cherries Exploding Under Pressure

My lips spoke in intricate patterns making her soul burn.
My tongue was uneducated in the art of inhibition.
It forced her heart, her soul and her spirit to listen.
She smiled I could hear her clitoris wishing,
for more of my oral tutorial, labia majora twisting,
so deep and subtle, wet intoxicating with its kissing.
I spoke in the form of my ancestral tongue,
with base like Mandingoes my words hung.
I told her of my ability to feel her flesh, her heart and her soul completely.
How with each stroke all lies would be broken discretely.
I warned her it would come in the form of screams.
It would be the sex of her dreams, she would always remember these things.
I was not her first, however, I was the first to make her burst.
I was the first to change her swears and curses.
Change them from spoken words to uncontrolled,
primal screams from deep in her soul.
It would be stimulation beyond comprehension this type of tension from my male extension.

Wet Cherries Exploding Under Pressure

She was so wet from my vocal effect,
I could swim in her love and be lost in her sweat.
Her clothes broke from her skin and she begged me to come in.
Her words broke from her heart as she expressed her duress.
From then on she could not be understood as I tempted her thighs.
As I watched tears roll from her eyes.
With each stroke I answered her whys.
Deep strokes uncovered all lies.
Sweat…Cum…Screams…Shaking
broken buttons, vaginal spasms.
I completely filled her chasm her arms so tightly around me in a fashion
beyond her control.
She spoke from beyond her soul.
Pulling me deeper not wanting to let go.
She was my canvas I painted ecstasy on her physicality.
I painted reality beyond her wildest fantasies.
She gave me her trust as I spoke the truth with each thrust.
When all was said and done she did not refuse to relinquish her cum.
She would never again be numb because she gave of herself all not some!

Personal

You have agitated my groin, my body, my mind, my soul and spirit to higher forms of expression so I explode at your lesson. You have pushed my stamina, my lust, my like, my want to new heights. I am in the stratosphere where my explosions are perversions held dear. You have taken what should be mild and made it hot, steaming, boiling, Caliente!

You have allowed me to push deep inside you without fear, knowing that when I am flowing no one can come near...

Personal.

You have taken my freak, my freaky, my dirty, my perverted to the point of no return. Oh so softly I touch you, firm, until your body erupts. I am stuck, no I am sticking to your tight womb wrapped around my manhood, thick, long, good. She rides the wood with conviction. Trying to tempt my heart to listen, but it has already heard her moans as she hides her face and her juicy lips that are sucked on when I am on. Her soft skin smells of some fruit or flower never too strong and always perfect...

Personal.

You have allowed my freak, my aggression to push until something comes out, you know what I am talking about. Exploit my body. Use my sex, my lips, my back, my dick, every inch I have to give and I will always have extra that is your privilege. To squirm, to squirt, to explode as your lips converse their pleasure and stretch to my measure. You move, you shake with no control, I pass the depth of your cervix, to your heart, your lungs, your head...

Personal.

I Dream of You

I dream of you.
I dream of things to do to you.
Washing your skin,
being your lover, your friend.
Holding you tight,
making you scream all night.
Tasting your lips,
being there when you are mad and want to flip.
I would fight for you.
Anything to get through to you,
if you don't believe then let me prove it to you.
Let me hug away the pain,
kiss away the doubt that lurks in your brain.
Give you the strength to love unrestrained.

I dream of you.
Wanting to touch my face,
wanting to be in my place.
How you wish to kiss my pain away,
be there if I needed you all day.
Rub my back,
best of all I wouldn't have to ask.
You'd kiss my lips,
whisper your heart in my ear,
take away this fear.
Please hear me.
I want you to long to be near me,
long to hear me.

I Dream of You

I dream of you.
I sleep fully at ease.
I long for your embrace.
Don't leave we can achieve
amazing things if you just love me.
Let your guard down
you've been hurt,
we can make it work.
I will never cheat,
never disrespect you.
Will you protect me? 'Cause I'd damn sure protect you.

I dream of you.

Wanting to touch me so much your heart aches,
never being fake,
there when I wake,
I dream of you.

I Wish I Could

I wish I could take away any doubt
that ails your soul. I wish I could remove the hurt,
loosen its hold. I wish I could see your smile. I wish
I could hold you if only for a while. I wish I could place at your feet, rose petals so soft underneath. I wish for you I could change the cold, make a smile on your lips so bold. I wish you knew the truth about you, how beautiful you are, you shine, you're a star. I wish the pain you hide would just die then I could see the happiness in your eyes. I wish I could go back in time, to stop you from falling, can't you hear me calling? No!

I wish the world could see past your pain, I would love to see you bring sunshine in the rain. I wish I could take all the bad you feel within my soul and shelter you. You make the sky blue, it's true. I wish just for once in your life you'd realize the truth, how beautiful you are just ask Langston Hughes. I wish I could send you the good that makes you smile every day, like the sun chasing the night away. I wish I could change all the things you feel, burn the bad so you would embrace your will.

I wish I could but I know I can't, so I'll watch you grow from so far back. You are so strong you'll break those chains, you'll kill that pain, so I wish you luck and blessings in everything.

Something Else

She loves me, she wants me and she needs me.

Her walk is ever flowing, got me ever growing, but y'all not knowing.

Her body is sculpted by the hands of Gods and Christs,

Oh yeah beans and rice and ladies nights,

Where she dances to the African drums,

Every sway of her hips the African drums,

Every push of her lips the African drums,

Every step from her feet, the African drums,

Every blink of her eyes the earth stops turning,

Just to recognize.

Something Else

When she exhales it's the coolest breeze on the hottest day,

Pushing all the bad things away.

By the way,

Her walk is the dance of seduction,

But never of destruction,

Only of life,

Of new beginnings,

Happy endings,

Her smile like the sun lights my dark world, Hum!

She's something else.

Never Knew Love but I Can Wish

I saw her on the crossroads between the dirty path of Africa and the paved streets of California. Her hair was chocolate brown, skin moist with the want of men, shining with the lust of sin. Her breasts were round like ripe cantaloupe with a chocolate soft skin. Her breasts were more than a mouth full, more than a hand full, but just right for me. She is my addiction, afro wearing, about the hate never caring. She has a cool demeanor, but man she be swearing. When she looks at me I want to tear my heart out and just to give it to her, however she does not want me to hurt myself.

We stand side by side her brown eyes so wide, her lips like honey so thick so sweet, her thighs like heaven and they only part for me. Her hands are so small so strong, so longing, so wanting and waiting. I found my get up and get down, in the town where Spanish Harlem meets Africa. I returned to the motherland in the house where the dirt roads meet the streets paved in gold. She is my Mount Zion, my nirvana. One kiss from her lips enlightens me beyond the physical limitation that once existed.

She is my head, I'm her locks twisted. I am her idea of perfection, her ideal erection, her ultimate protection in this process of physical attraction. I am her only thought and she is my only breath. I lay at her ass…set in a way that her body is an hour glass. My love for her is bitter, so much so that I cry when I am not with her. She is my craving with no limits or boundaries.

I've never known love, true love but this is my idea of it.

Butterfly Effect

The flap of her wings, her hips, her thighs, the blink of life's existence caught in her eyes. The wisdom you can see that accents her beauty. The elegance and grace, how she walks and that face she makes changes the world. If she smiles at me then everyone I pass will feel the urge to laugh. My day is made by her kindness. Think that if just for one moment her finest is sent to me bringing the joy I see. Butterfly effect!

The movement of her cheeks to form a smile for me, the touch of her hand on my arm brings me joy. She has such class and charm. I am at a loss for words but I am strengthened by her lack of words. It is so absurd how she controls without controlling, how she holds without confinement or pressure. She is an enigma, an action that cannot be stopped. She is forever in someone's heart. Butterfly effect!

The way she makes me feel, she is soul for real. Be her skin white like snow or black like onyx, she moves someone, something, somewhere even when she is not aware. She is the beauty of a sunny day. She is the personified emotion of a stormy night. Her butterfly kisses change my good from bad, my happy from sad, my fear to bravery, my freedom from slavery. She is truth saving me from the lies I pursue. Butterfly effect!

She is the reason that wars will be fought, that against all odds we will not come up short. She is the birth giver. If not mother, sister, lover, friend, teacher, preacher, then the things in this world that I am and can be she is so much more. She is African pride before hate arrived, she is the part of our culture that we thought did not survive and yet she is alive. Butterfly effect!

What She Needs

I want to tear off her clothes,
have her flesh exposed,
make her body fold.
Black chrome diamond sex beyond rationale.
Make her mind experience dementia.
Her voice explode in a primal scream,
because I am in between her heart and lungs.
I want to touch her hair and pull her back,
to let her know I'm there.
I want to suck all her juices from her quivering,
shivering, shaking,
so hard back breaking.
Eyes wild in a frenzy,
saying "how you got all that in me?"
Passion beyond earth, heaven, time,
I'm holding her close as she explodes in my arms,
telling me she can't breathe, too much pleasure she's alarmed. I say "You do not need to breathe,
I will supply your breath."
Her eyes cannot focus.
Our lust, love, touch, fuck, suck, lick, intertwined bodies so ferocious.
No understandable words come from her lips,
Only cum from in between her hips.
She is my canvas on which I've drawn my love's lust,
precise force as I thrust,
I swirl,
Oh damn girl,
she has the world.

What She Needs

Listening to her explosions,
I am a writer composing,
symphonies of love on naked flesh.
She grips my arms,
her love so warm, so hot, so much energy,
I've got nothing to lose in this place. She tries to get
away, I pull her back and say,
"This is mine."
Her wild eyes agree.
Though her throat says only screams,
I understand what she means.
Her body leaks love with no hesitance,
her lips kiss mine with no resistance.
Her eyes cry joy so relentless,
she explodes over and over and over until,
each orgasm becomes one continuous,
Explosion of her lust.
I will not let her go,
my goal is to make her cum

One

More

Time.
Of all that I want to do to you,
I see what is there in you.
She don't need someone trying to have sex with her.
She needs a friend who will be true.
So for her this I will do...Because it is what she needs.

Diamond Rings

I value her thoughts, her intellect, the way she rolls her hips and neck. Not in anger, not in a stereotypical clause but when she grooves. The sounds that soothe and the sexy way she be looking at me. She moves my groin not with her hips but the words that come from her lips. Her words make it easier to watch the movement of her lips. She is beyond comprehension. I am enchanted with her sleekness. She is my perfect melody giving these words that I express so much more interest, even without her caress I am obliterated by her yes!

Will you be my wife to have and to hold when days are sunny or dark and cold? Through thick and thin, through the strongest wind till our hearts say the end? Damn she can call me to arms with her wit and charms. She is like a swarm of honey bees producing sweetness in the trees. She has the softest spoken strength, awoken thought provoking equal to and maybe beyond me and you. She is not afraid of her sexuality, she does not judge another's reality only states sweetheart it isn't for me. Those who are smart walk away and let it be.

She is that gangster...to that gangster. She is that main...to that pimp. Naw man she is much more to them. Standing outside of the old hymns sung by aging lips she is the culture from her hips to her feet and from her lips come such sweet verses of me. She is consumed with my wellness not my well endowments. She is not afraid of trueness or closeness. She does not fear me she knows I will not be a chain to her. She knows I will never want to control her. She knows I only want to hold, not hold her down. I am not a weight holding her to the ground and she sees this.

I Covet

Looking at your lips...
I want to kiss them for the longest while.
You must stop the world every time your lips smile.
I enjoy your face, your hair, you have so much style.
You are a queen in training.
For you there is so much time remaining.
You are so beautiful.

You are so much like what a woman should do.
You should be the model they look up too.
I enjoy your honesty.
How you long to talk to me.
I do the same.
There's even beauty in your name.
Look at you trying to move the world.
Can I help you?
I'm lost in you girl.
I know this may seem like just words from the start.
But every time I type a line baby I am giving you my heart.
I covet...

Holding you so tight I am squeezing you.
Kissing you each touch of my lips I am pleasing you.
Doing things to,
your precious body but only if you want me to.

I Covet

Tasting your skin,
My arms holding you so tight you loose your wind.
I am the act of being your lover, your friend.
Moving this love with what we got within.
I want to give you poetry every day,

Kissing you so much your smile never goes away.
I hear your heart beat, when I hold you close.
It means so much to me.
Would you come to me?
Would you cum for me?
Would you cry tears of joy?
While my love fills your void?
I covet...

Letting you know, this is more than physical.
This thing we have is more than anatomical, more than
spiritual. I covet cooking you dinner,
running your bath,
holding you close and telling you jokes to make you laugh.
This must be witchcraft.
Let me speak to your heart through the words from my lips.

Allow my lust to taste your soul and never be apart,
I covet...

Being happy with you!

Can I Take You Out Sometime?

I saw you sitting over there looking all retro with twists in your hair. You sat as if you didn't have a care. Damn, I wanted to get up the nerve to approach you and profess not my love but your loveliness. I wanted to express what you convey to me in that earth tone dress. I wanted to relay how damn! your flyness is so vaness. What does that mean? Oh! It is just another word for damn you are the word. Baby you are the jelly, hot toast and jam. In fact the whole breakfast, lunch and dinner with fine wine. You convey in that dress how you blow my mind, how you move my soul, you are all women and seeing you is like seeing an omen. Can I advance and talk to you? Oh yes I know you don't know me and you look so content. You are so like the wind in the midst of trees bent, unseen and still a presence. Baby you are like so much money you can never be spent. I just want to know can I come and talk to you? Can I see what's on your beautiful mind that forms your lips in the shape of a smile? Can I hear your voice and be a part of your choice? I don't have the courage to do it, so I just watch from afar like a scientist studying a distant star. Damn sister can I come over? Baby you move my lips to smile when this world gets me down. I wonder what you're drinking. It's got to be the best wine.

n k o t o ti

You are so retro, you are so fine like a Mona Lisa for this time. So can I come over? Maybe sit for a while? I promise not to bother you or cramp your style. I am like a moth to a flame wanting to feel the pain of your touch, wanting to burn in your glow, even if it's in your no. So can I come over like an R&B song sung so strong? I want to be next to you, damn I don't need to have sex with you. Just be chosen to be next to you, but in truth I do want to. Can I come over? Hey, one last thing can I talk to your heart just for a minute? Maybe a spark but by the time I've finished you will have a new tattoo. No, not one seen with the eyes but if you touch the inner thighs my mark will be left inside. Can I come over, just for a minute just to introduce the cool that is I? The fool that is I, and just ask the universe why and how did it make the beautiful that is you so strong, so sexy? You are so retro, so lively so much of a monolith a timeless look never spent or out of fashion, you are fashion. You are everlasting throughout time smashing. I am humbly asking, Can I come over just to be in your presence?

Can I come over?

You

Damn, I look into your eyes and I want to smile.
I love your lips, your skin, your hair, your style.
You are the cool in the hot summer breeze,
making the hard world at ease.
When I look at you I think
he is so lucky, so cool, he must be a god of some sort
to have attracted you.
I smile,
all the while,
captivated by your ways and style.
You are that satisfying meal,
Baby Face must have met you when he wrote *Whip Appeal.*
You make money obsolete,
you are black gold and platinum,
you shine when you walk these streets.
You are a million out of a possible ten,
trying to open up your heart and let someone in.
They don't deserve you,
because they are a burden to you,
but you choose to give them your love,
because you choose to give them you.
You are so precious,
while I am not a Christian,
there is a god because it has blessed us,
with you.

You Move

You move my mouth to speak the truth out.
I am weak in your presence but strong with no doubt.
I would give you my heart but you already possess it.
I would tell you how I feel but you already know.
You make my heart beat fast, with your chocolate mind.
You are so strong, so independent, so little and so fine.
You remind me of nothing you are new.
You look like nothing because you are incomparably beautiful.
Your lips taste like nothing on earth they are too sweet.
Your body is my book each word I will read.
I will move at your pace.
Slow, fast, in between the lips on your face.
Tell me what you want I will give it.
Tell what you need, I will provide it.
When I hear your voice I feel like two hearts united.
I love what I feel, I promise I won't fight it.
Just as long as you remain real we can be undivided.
Will you be all mine? I am yours all decided.
Uncontrolled emotional explosion.
You move me to create life from my head to my fingertips. Look what you have created, something beautiful. You move me to sounds and the way you feel I am so astounded. I would fight an army for you and no man could take me down. I want to know your deepest secrets even the ones of fear and shame. I want to be the one you call if you need someone to blame. You move me to honesty, honestly!

Speak to Me

Baby I know it's all just words especially when your heart breaks,

But like they say don't let me pay for his damn mistakes.

I offer you nothing you can buy in a store,

My heart, my soul, my dreams, my goals, tell me if you need more.

She undressed her mind and let me into her soul,

Deep desires as lust and love. Sweating, things unfold.

It's no longer too cold as we intertwine so deeply,

So literally, as we touch with our mind's hands,

And…

Then I touch and she touches me with her body's hands,

She is not afraid of love.

She may have baggage but she carries it well,

I'd follow her to heaven and be in heaven with her in hell,

She is my vanilla, I mean

Mocha,

Chocolate,

Speak to Me

Sexy, thick, thin, keeping these words coming, my beautiful...no.

My seductive...no.

She is so much more than all my words and yet,

She is my words.

She wants me to touch her flesh she knows my heart,

She wants to be lost in loves sweat.

Simply no words can describe the physical part,

She is not afraid to speak on a higher plane,

She knows my fears, my words, my pain,

She knows that my only goal is to gain her love.

She is not afraid of my physical touch,

It is beyond words of ultimate trust.

We can speak poetry for eternity,

Never expressing the truth that is this,

We can make love for days and she believes in me.

She knows I will get it. Speak to me.

I Want to Fuck You Senseless

I want to fuck you blind so you can see with the eyes of your mind. I want to fuck you till your throat is dry. I want to fuck you until your eyes cry tears of joy. I want to fuck you for eternity, so deep your pain forever sleeps in my soul. I want to fuck you until you loose control. I want to fuck you until your soul is free, then when you look up at me, eyes wild, pussy exploding uncontrollably asking, "Why me?" I want to fuck you until the answer comes through. Until I say, "'Cause of all the women I knew, you deserve the fucking I do." I want to fuck you until your organs begin to cum.

I want to fuck you until you try to get away so I can pull your hair and say, "Oh! No, bitch don't run!" I want to fuck you so that even when I'm dead and gone your flesh will still be cumin, damn I got it going on. I want to fuck you until you reach evolution, until you reach the sky. I want to fuck you until you OD you'll be just that high. I want to fuck you till your body loses all its strength and goes weak. I want to start fucking you on Friday and keep going until next week.

I want to fuck you senseless.

Until your "oh shits" and "damns" can no longer be understood. I want to fuck you in the suburbs until we reach the deepest hood. I want to fuck you until you understand how much you move my soul. I want to grab your hair and bend you back until your eyes begin to roll.

I Want to Fuck You Senseless

I want to fuck you until you feel me in your chest, head, heart and soul. I want to hold your convulsing body and tell you let the pain go. I want to fuck you until all your problems leave your head. I want to fuck you back to life because right now your soul is dead. I want to lick, stick, and suck until you gag on my love. I want to fuck you until you cum from just a hug.

I want to fuck you senseless.

I want to fuck you until you realize that I mean every word I speak. Listen Miss in all trueness no mistakes were made when you blessed me with your kiss. I want to fuck you until I remove all doubt. I know you got a lot on your plate but I can fuck all the bad shit out. I want to fuck you for all the time you gave and did not receive. I want to fuck you till your body breaks and your lungs can't breathe. I want to fuck you until you believe, until your body has been freed.

Energy Flow

Breathe for today you will realize what has never been told to you. Today you will see what has never been exposed to you. Today you will remember your life before conception, a world of pure energy and no deception. Today your movement will cease to stop. You will flow through eternity with nothing to hinder you. Forever connected with all things so no matter what you do all things will remember you.

Today's Thought

I thought today I am not an animal, not a mad flesh eating cannibal. I am not y'all understand, my logic is always by your standards flawed. I thought, I am not the man you see, but I am the man before me, then I thought I am not a man at all, and I will never be the one to fall. I thought if life is abundant, then that means within this circumference, there must be life immense. I thought if the road less traveled is said to be correct, then the road not traveled is worthy of respect. I thought if life is so important when it is gone and flesh is all that's left, does nothing have importance in the face of death? I thought if she ignores me to get my attention, and I ignore her for lack of attention, who wins and when does it end? I thought nothing, and for the first time came up with something, that I've been thinking too much and acting too little.

Dance

I am music hear my rhythm. Unforgiving sounds freed like piano keys,

Blown like trumpets allowing me to breathe.

I will free tempos from drums, bongos to cymbals.

My written words are so nimble so quick.

Listen how they jump from my fingertips, from my vocal cords to my

Chocolate lips.

Then in a leap of death to your virgin ears and you ain't heard shit.

I am written, spoken, imitating Art Tatum, blowing my Louie Armstrong

Notes so high.

Vocal power Mahalia Jackson making Christians cry.

I am the chromatic scale each and every note exhaled.

Minors, majors, sharps to flat, guitar strings strummed along with

High hats.

Dance!

I am the ballet, rhythm, Cubano, Africano precision,

Written down to the sound of freedom wanted now!

Dance

How can you deny me rhythm so free, tuned precisely with

Each key?

Do Re Mi

Fah Sol La Ti

Full whole steps in the spectrum of sound kept in close proximity to me.

I am the living metronome. Sound clone and yet I stand still alone.

This dance my tongue does a Billie Holliday, a Cab Calloway, a Marvin Gaye.

And at the same time a hint of Mel Tome, and I am Sinatra, bold enough I

Did it my way.

Until these word notes I wrote went flat back to black, blues rhythm and

Soul.

I Nat King Cole, did a switch with my soul, straightened my hair, dawned a

Tux and sang away my despair.

Dance!

Move Me

She moves me. Her skin, darkened peanut butter, smooth to the eye, soft to the touch. It is her deepened, yet soft womanly voice, her breast, her stomach the small of her back so beautiful. It is her backside, her deep, dark, oval eyes. The possibility that she may like me, maybe more. She moves me.

Music moves me. The soft introduction of a melodic chord. It is the passion that each note possesses, yet in comparison to the whole piece, insignificant. Oh of course it is the joy, sad or mad emotional state that can be evoked by the truly talented musician. These masters being so in touch with their own emotions convey their ideas easily. Music moves me.

My family moves me. To anger to joy and all the in betweens. My family inspires me to words, to write, to fight, to sing. They move me to closeness. They move me to be open. They move me to know that even in my stupidity my ability to choose is still untouched. Why? Because I chose them and I will always choose them as they chose me. My family moves me.

I Wish

I wish I had known this a long time ago

That I was chocolate platinum with diamond brown eyes

Coarse black pearl hair

The mind of infinite wisdom

I wish I had seen me for me

Not for what they wanted me to see

You know the doubt and his brother and sisters self hate and self denial

And their cousins aunts nieces and nephews

Bringing you such bad news

I wish they would just decay

They

Are what I wish to go away

But no genie

Is here to do magic tricks for me

To push this hate from the air that I breathe, I only wish I could see

What is truly there in me

I wish

I Am

I am tasty chocolate with a tad bit of strawberry, come and taste me.

Stronger than the lion, a monolith but damn woman you move me.

I am skin soft as satin, smooth as silk, black chrome chocolate milk.

Come, hold me. I am not cold, I am not anger, I am not lost I am found.

You are a paradox of flesh unparalleled. I am not him. My love does not seek to own just to love, my love does not want your heart, it does not want your head, or even your time. Well just a few seconds of your acknowledgement, or maybe some day to be in your presence even if just to say, "Hi."

I Am

I am the king of the African soldiers one in infinite I promise. Let me into your pictures, your still frame, that dark happiness that some call pain. I am the sweetest juice and all who taste me are lost in blessed happiness. I am lack of stress, let me relax your stress. I can tell a queen, so your highness I am forever blessed, trying to say the "write" words to get in your nest. I know you protest, but I am ease, calm, storming excitement. I am all desire flesh, spirit, head. I am life for the dying, my love could raise the dead, I am the soldier, last of my kind. My love is not a cage of the body or mind, I will not confine you. I will not hold you my love is just an extra boost of power to take you closer to what you want. You are my breakfast at Tiffany's, my dove from its cage. I am freedom let your wings rest on me and never be weary.

Freedom

Sometimes I wake in the morning as sun shines on my chocolate skin, I think of you and I
smile. There is no pain in this place I am...experiencing freedom. I look in the mirror and I
love the lips, the eyes, the nose, the ears that are before me. I am experiencing...love for
myself.
Sometimes I hold my own hand, remembering that patience is the key. I touch my own face
'cause damn I love me. This is more than black pride, like a happy, joyful roller coaster ride
my heart is experiencing...freedom.
I have shed enough tears, I will shed no more. I will devour the world and regurgitate
creativity on a level never seen before. I have been experiencing...happiness. For the first time
I am consumed not with what I lack but what I will gain back, with self love. I am
experiencing...freedom.
Sometimes I look in the sky and see birds so high, if we live with purpose then doubt can't hurt
us! I am experiencing...wisdom. Words set to music, words start wars and words have so much
power so what will I use them for? I am experiencing...enlightenment.
Sometimes I wake in the morning and smile, not because of what I have, but because I am me
and there
is none like me unique, with my own power, loved, hated, befriended, I am
experiencing...freedom.

A Note to the World

Please let me live. Unshackle these chains and allow me to grow.

Don't suck my life dry and kill my dreams slowly.

If I may see beyond my potential death do not bury me in hate,

Until nothing is left.

Culture my garden please don't salt my earth.

Fill my lungs with love of life it is mine for my making,

Yet you have applied the lot of these straws and now my back is breaking.

Please cultivate my essence show me peace, show me humanity.

Do not fall on my life like flooding rain bringing me strife.

A Note to the World

Grow me, give me plenty of sun.

Teach me, allow me to be educated in happiness.

Sing sweetly my heart to sleep and allow me to wake with plenty to eat.

If you wish to drown me let it be in positivity.

Show my eyes the good in all things, hide me from the bad that life brings.

Dance with me and show me I am beautiful without conditions or strings.

If possible consider me a note to the world.

Less Traveled the Road

If love and hate are the only things in life I will choose neither. If hot and cold are our only sensations then I will choose not to feel. If good and evil are our only ways, I will again simply decline the choice and in that instant maybe hear the truly enlightened voice. If God and the Devil are the only things to worship, I will choose not to worship at all. I will choose to step outside of my little ball and I may fail but maybe not. Yet if failure and success are the only outcomes I will simply choose neither. Maybe I will choose complacency. If righteousness and sin our only human achievements I will choose nothing at all, neither in between them nor in opposition to them. If beauty is the ruler that ugly is judged by I will simply not use the ruler I have been given. If I am told lust or love I will fold, because I will refuse to be trained and then maybe outside of my given possibilities find truth. I will do. Not try. Not succeed, just do and let whatever comes to pass me be. Only then will I wonder and only will it matter if I did my best. However, I then would wonder if doing my best is the answer or if just doing is the key.

Thinking outside of this reality.

COMING SOON

CHRONICLES OF THE BLACK CASTLE

LAST CONFESSIONS - LAST CONFESSION NEW BODY

CHILDREN OF LAOS-RISE OF AHSIA

RUN AWAY WITH ME

BY SYLVESTER S. WRIGHT

www.ingramcontent.com/pod-product-compliance
Lightning Source LLC
LaVergne TN
LVHW010111170826
845678LV00012B/2349

* 9 7 9 8 8 1 3 5 8 1 5 7 1 *